Why Do We Need Rocks and Minerals?

Kelley MacAulay

Crabtree Publishing Company

www.crabtreebooks.com

Author
Kelley MacAulay

Publishing plan research and development
Reagan Miller

Notes to adults
Reagan Miller

Editor
Crystal Sikkens

Proofreader
Wendy Scavuzzo

Design
Tammy McGarr

Photo research
Tammy McGarr, Crystal Sikkens

**Production coordinator
and prepress technician**
Tammy McGarr

Print coordinator
Margaret Amy Salter

Photographs
Dreamstime: page 5
Photo courtesy photos-public-domain.com: page 8
Thinkstock: page 24 (magma)
All other images by Shutterstock

Library and Archives Canada Cataloguing in Publication

MacAulay, Kelley, author
    Why do we need rocks and minerals / Kelley MacAulay.

(Natural resources close-up)
Includes index.
Issued in print and electronic formats.
ISBN 978-0-7787-0492-8 (bound).--ISBN 978-0-7787-0496-6 (pbk.).--
ISBN 978-1-4271-8217-3 (html).--ISBN 978-1-4271-8221-0 (pdf)

    1. Rocks--Juvenile literature. 2. Minerals--Juvenile literature.
3. Mines and mineral resources--Juvenile literature. I. Title.

QE365.2.M23 2014   j549   C2014-900380-3
                                      C2014-900381-1

Library of Congress Cataloging-in-Publication Data

MacAulay, Kelley, author.
  Why do we need rocks and minerals? / Kelley MacAulay.
      pages cm. -- (Natural resources close-up)
    Includes index.
    ISBN 978-0-7787-0492-8 (reinforced library binding : alk. paper) -- ISBN 978-
0-7787-0496-6 (pbk. : alk. paper) -- ISBN 978-1-4271-8217-3 (electronic html)
-- ISBN 978-1-4271-8221-0 (electronic pdf)
    1. Rocks--Juvenile literature. 2. Minerals--Juvenile literature. 3. Natural
resources--Juvenile literature. I. Title.

    QE432.2.M225 2014
    553--dc23
                            2014002278

Crabtree Publishing Company

Printed in the USA/052014/SN20140313

www.crabtreebooks.com   1-800-387-7650

Published in Canada
Crabtree Publishing
616 Welland Ave.
St. Catharines, Ontario
L2M 5V6

Published in the United States
Crabtree Publishing
PMB 59051
350 Fifth Avenue, 59th Floor
New York, New York 10118

Published in the United Kingdom
Crabtree Publishing
Maritime House
Basin Road North, Hove
BN41 1WR

Published in Australia
Crabtree Publishing
3 Charles Street
Coburg North
VIC 3058

Contents

Rocks are resources

People use things found in nature. These things are called natural resources. Air, water, and trees are natural resources. Trees can give us food to eat, such as apples, and wood to burn for heat.

Rocks and minerals are natural resources. They make up the land on Earth. We use them every day! Rocks are used to make homes and schools. Minerals in your toothpaste keep your teeth clean.

Many minerals

There are more than 3,000 minerals on Earth! We dig minerals out of the ground. Minerals are found in rocks. They can be very colorful. Minerals are made up of tiny **crystals**.

mineral fluorite

diamond

Minerals have **properties**. Properties describe
something, such as how it looks and feels.
One property of a mineral might be how hard
it is. Some minerals are harder than others.
Diamonds are the hardest minerals on Earth!

Made of minerals

Rocks are made up of minerals. Some rocks are made of one mineral. Others are made of more than one mineral. The rock known as pegmatite is often made up of the minerals quartz, feldspar, and mica.

mica (black)

feldspar (pink)

quartz (gray)

What do you think?

Rocks come in all shapes and sizes. **Boulders** are the biggest pieces of rock. Clay is made from the tiniest pieces of rock. Pebbles and sand are in between. Which are bigger rock pieces, pebbles or sand?

boulder

pebbles

sand

Building new rocks

There are three types of rocks. Each type forms in a different way. One type of rock is made from little pieces of rock that are pressed together. First, rivers and streams break away pieces of rock.

Then the pieces of rock build up into layers. Each layer presses down on the layer below it. The layers become very hard and form new rock. The Grand Canyon in Arizona is made from this type of rock.

Heat and pressure

Another type of rock is made from **magma**. Magma is hot liquid rock inside Earth. When magma reaches Earth's surface it is called **lava**. New rock forms when lava cools and hardens.

new rock

lava

The third type of rock is formed deep inside Earth. This rock is heated until the minerals change. A new type of rock forms, when the minerals change. Marble is an example of this type of rock.

marble

Worn by weather

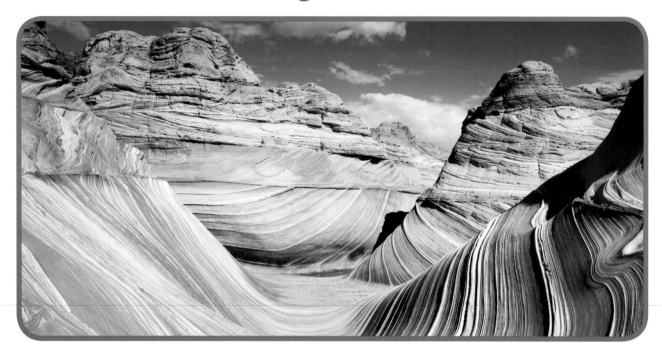

Rocks are broken up by weather. Rain and strong winds hitting rocks breaks them into pieces. Rocks can form beautiful shapes as they wear down.

Very tiny pieces of broken rock form new **soil**. Soil is a loose material on Earth's surface. Plants grow in soil. Plants provide food for living things.

soil

Everyday resources

We use things every day that come from rocks and minerals. Salt is a mineral that flavors our food. **Gems**, such as rubies and emeralds, are beautiful minerals used to make jewelry.

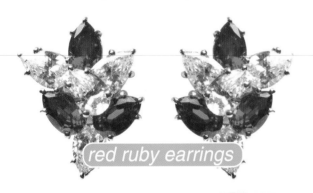

red ruby earrings

green emerald ring

salt

Pencil lead comes from the mineral graphite. Sand is used to make glass for things such as windows and eyeglasses. Pottery is made from clay.

What do you think?

Sand and clay are both made from rock pieces. Which one contains larger pieces of rock? (See page 9 for help.)

clay pottery bowl

17

Many metals

Metals are common minerals found in rocks. Many types of metals are used every day. Gold, silver, copper, aluminum, and iron are some examples of metals. Gold and silver are used to make jewelry.

silver

gold

Aluminum is used for making soda cans, pots, and pans. Copper is used for making coins. Some metals can be mixed together to make other metals. Copper and tin are used to make bronze.

aluminum cans

copper coins

gold medal

silver medal

bronze medal

Reduce

There are only so many rocks and minerals on Earth. Once they are used, it could take millions of years before new rocks and minerals form. It is important to use these natural resources wisely.

digging for iron

Rocks and minerals have to be dug out of the ground. This can harm the plants, animals, and even people that live nearby. Reducing, or using less, of these natural resources cuts down on the amount that needs to be dug from the ground.

digging for granite

Reuse and recycle

Reusing can also help save rocks and minerals. To reuse means to use something again. Instead of throwing away old glass jars, you could use them to store small items, such as buttons.

Recycling is taking something old and turning it into something new. Glass jars and aluminum cans can be recycled into new jars and cans.

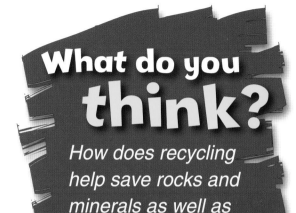

What do you think?

How does recycling help save rocks and minerals as well as the environment?

Metal

Glass

Words to know

 boulders 9

 **crystals** 6

 gems 16

lava 12

 **magma** 12

properties 7

soil 15

Notes to adults and an activity

This activity lets children practice their sorting skills and get a close-up look at different rocks and minerals.

Materials: a collection of different rocks

Procedure

1. Discuss the different words we use to describe rocks (dull, shiny, big, small, rough, smooth, soft, hard)
2. Provide a collection of rocks to children.
3. Give children time to observe the rocks and sort them in groups.
4. Allow each group to present their rocks to others and explain their sorting rules.

Learning More

Books

Rock Study: A Guide to Looking at Rocks by Steve M. Hoffman. Rosen Publishing Group, 2011.

National Geographic Readers: Rocks and Minerals by Kathleen Weidner Zoehfeld. National Geographic Society, 2012.

Websites

This website has several informative links; including one that provides examples of familiar household items made from minerals.
www.mineralogy4kids.org/

This kid-friendly site covers topics related to geology and includes video links, games, and activity ideas.
www.canadiangeographic.ca/cgKidsAtlas/rock.asp

This site includes engaging and informative links that explain the rock cycle and how to safely collect rocks.
http://fi.edu/fellows/fellow1/rocks/index2.html